SOLVING REAL-WORLD PROBLEMS WITH CHEMICAL ENGINEERING

DON RAUF

Britannica
Educational Publishing

IN ASSOCIATION WITH

ROSEN
EDUCATIONAL SERVICES

Published in 2016 by Britannica Educational Publishing (a trademark of Encyclopædia Britannica, Inc.) in association with The Rosen Publishing Group, Inc.
29 East 21st Street, New York, NY 10010

Distributed exclusively by Rosen Publishing.
To see additional Britannica Educational Publishing titles, go to rosenpublishing.com.

First Edition

Britannica Educational Publishing
J.E. Luebering: Director, Core Reference Group
Mary Rose McCudden: Editor, Britannica Student Encyclopedia

Rosen Publishing
Hope Lourie Killcoyne: Executive Editor
Nicholas Croce: Editor
Nelson Sá: Art Director
Michael Moy: Designer
Cindy Reiman: Photography Manager
Sherri Jackson: Photo Researcher

Library of Congress Cataloging-in-Publication Data

Rauf, Don, author.
 Solving real world problems with chemical engineering / Don Rauf.
    pages cm. -- (Let's find out! Engineering)
Audience: Grades 1 to 4.
 Includes bibliographical references and index.
 ISBN 978-1-68048-265-2 (library bound) — ISBN 978-1-5081-0077-5 (pbk.) — ISBN 978-1-68048-322-2 (6-pack)

1. Chemical engineering--Juvenile literature. 2. Clean energy--Juvenile literature. I. Title.
TP155.R35 2016
660--dc23
                                                                                              2015033912

Manufactured in the United States of America

CONTENTS

WHAT IS CHEMICAL ENGINEERING?

If you take a close look at the world around you, you will see the work of chemical engineers: plastic bottles, disposable diapers, gasoline, clothes, makeup, bubble gum. Chemical engineers develop products that are used every day, from the fuel in your car to the plastic container that holds your lunch.

Some people call chemical engineers magicians because they

Chemical engineers create materials such as plastics. They also improve existing products. For example, some newer plastics break down faster in landfills.

THINK ABOUT IT

Chemical engineers often work with atoms and molecules. Molecules are atoms bonded together. Atoms and molecules are very small. People can see them only with powerful microscopes. What is the smallest thing you have ever seen?

can change substances. For example, to make car tires stronger, chemical engineers have created new forms of rubber. Rubber comes from trees, but chemical engineers can improve it to make it perform better.

These engineers use science to solve real-world problems. They make products, such as laundry detergent and automobiles, safer for the environment and easier to use. Chemical engineers need to be experts in chemistry, biology, mathematics, and physics.

Salt is an example of a widely used natural chemical compound.

How to Blow a Better Bubble

Whenever you blow a bubble with chewing gum, you are seeing the work of a chemical engineer. Chewing gum goes back to the days of ancient civilizations. People chewed on thick sweet tree sap to freshen their breath and to clean their teeth. In the Americas, the Aztec and Mayan civilizations chewed white gummy sap from the bark of an evergreen tree called the sapodilla. That sap is called chicle.

Chicle gum was introduced into the United States in the 1800s. In 1880 sugar flavoring was added and chewing gum became very popular. Gum

Scientists have developed synthetic gum bases that keep a sweet flavor and are chewy, stretchy, and elastic.

Polyethylene is a polymer. A polymer is a long chain of smaller molecules hooked together, almost like a long string of pearls. The smaller molecules are called monomers. Monomers can combine chemically to other molecules to form a polymer. Polyethylene is an artifical polymer, but polymers exist in nature as well. The most common natural polymer is cellulose, a natural material found in trees and plants.

companies soon learned that they would never have enough chicle to make the amount of gum people wanted. Chemical engineers came to the rescue. They determined that they could use polyethylene instead of chicle. Polyethylene is the most widely used plastic in the world. It has elastic properties, which allows bubble gum to stretch when blowing bubbles.

Plastic bags are typically made from polymers.

Here Comes the Sun—and Other Clean Energy

Many modern machines require energy to make them run. Most of this energy comes from sources that are not good for the environment. People would like to use energy sources that will keep the air cleaner and reduce global warming.

Solar technology uses the sun for energy. Chemical engineers have played an important role in improving ways to capture the sun's energy. They have designed the most efficient solutions for collecting solar energy and

As fossil fuel sources start to decrease, people are looking to the sun and wind to generate energy.

converting it to electricity.

Some chemical engineers have figured out how to use salts to store the sun's energy as heat. The traditional solar cells are made of crystalline silicon. These are silicon atoms connected together to form a crystal-like structure.

Chemical engineers have been working on new molecules to make organic solar cells. They also help create materials that help store and generate power from wind, tides, waves, and rivers.

Solar energy collection typically uses large flat panels.

COMPARE AND CONTRAST

How do you think solar energy is different from burning coal or gas?

Saving the Planet with Chemical Know-How

In the fight against pollution, chemical engineers have played an important role. In 1947 chemical engineer Vladimir Haensel figured out a way to use the element platinum to make gasoline that was cleaner, produced more energy, and cost less. Since then, chemists have found other ways to make cleaner-burning fuels.

For example, scientists can use hydrogen gas to lower the amounts of harmful lead and sulfur in gasoline and diesel fuel. Many cars

Chemical engineers have helped to reduce the pollutants in car exhaust.

THINK ABOUT IT

What are some problems in the environment that might be solved with chemical engineering?

have a device called a catalytic converter, invented by the chemical engineer John Mooney and the chemist Carl Keith. Pollutants in a car's exhaust are turned into harmless compounds after they have passed through the converter.

Chemical engineers have also come up with recycling methods for metals, paper, and plastic. Aluminum cans, for example, can be recycled through a special process to remove paint, labels, and impurities. Recycling these cans reduces air pollution and energy use compared to making new aluminum.

Through chemical engineering methods, aluminum can be recycled so it can be reused.

KEEPING CHIPS CRISPY AND BEYOND

Why is your potato chip so fresh and crisp? You may want to thank chemical engineers for that. Pringles® chips are actually made from a mix of dehydrated potato flakes, starch, and water. The mixture is made into a dough. From this dough, uniform curved chips are cut and fried. The identical chips stack perfectly in a tube, like one used for tennis balls.

Chemical engineers also played a role in developing the can, which keeps the chips fresh for a year or more. Each can is filled with nitrogen, which blocks

Chemistry helps keep potato chips crispy.

COMPARE AND CONTRAST
How do things taste if they are not kept in airtight containers?

exposure to oxygen. Also, the container blocks light, which can cause spoilage.

Chemical engineers have also helped to make food preservatives, food additives, and artificial sweeteners and flavors. They have created versions of foods that can be cooked quickly, such as rice and beans. These scientists have also come up with ways to preserve food, such as by flash freezing and freeze-drying.

One modern method of preserving food is freeze-drying. The process involves quickly freezing the food and then putting it in a vacuum-sealed bag. Many foods can be freeze-dried.

Silly Putty® and Other Fun Things

Boric acid is a white or colorless crystalline compound. It is used to make many things, from cement to cosmetics to poison. Silicone oil is the liquid form of the chemical silicone. It is used to make rubber and is used in plastic surgery.

It pays to play when you are in the world of chemistry. James Wright was an engineer at the General Electric Research Lab during World War II. He was searching for a way to make a cheaper synthetic rubber. One day he mixed boric acid with silicone oil. The combination

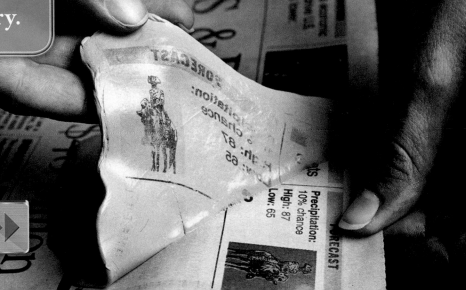

Silly Putty® was invented when trying to make a cheap type of rubber.

transformed into a material that stretched and bounced more than regular rubber. The new material also did something totally unexpected. When pressed against newspaper print, it picked up the ink.

The government did not see any use for his substance. But businessman Peter Hodgson saw how fun the product could be. He packaged it in a plastic egg because he began selling it around Easter. He sold it under the name of Silly Putty®. It went on to become one of the most popular toys of the 20th century.

The handiwork of chemical engineers can be seen in many toys when you think of how many are made of plastics and rubber.

Businessman Peter Hodgson realized the substance could make a fun toy.

A Sticky Situation

Some inventions come from accidents. Spencer Silver was a chemist with the company 3M. He was experimenting with different elements and compounds to make a super-strong glue to help build airplanes. He developed a sticky substance called acrylate copolymer microspheres. The material was not strong, but it could make paper stick to something temporarily.

The company was not sure how to use the product at first. Another 3M

The invention of the Post-It® note was another happy accident. A scientist trying to make a strong glue came up with a weak adhesive, which was perfect for temporarily sticking paper.

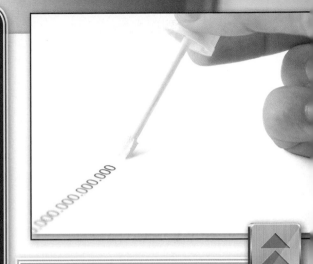

COMPARE AND CONTRAST

Sometimes mixing two things together will create something new. Can you think of two things you like to mix together? What do they make? (Like chocolate syrup and milk to make chocolate milk.) What are these things like separately? How do they change when mixed together?

Look around an office and you will probably find the work of the chemical engineer, such as correction fluid that covers writing errors.

employee—the chemical engineer Art Fry—found the answer. He sang in a church choir and wanted a way to mark pages without losing his place in the songbook. He used Silver's glue on pieces of paper. It worked so well that he began using it around the office as well. Once it became clear how useful the product could be, 3M started production. The Post-It® went on to become one of the company's most successful products.

MEDICAL MARVELS

People with heart trouble will sometimes have tubes called stents put in their body to make blood flow more easily. The material in these stents is chemically engineered to be both strong and lightweight.

Chemistry plays an important role in making materials that can help physical problems. Artificial knees and hips, for example, are made of substances combining polymers and a metal called titanium.

Chemical engineers may also help develop or improve medicines. Chemist Jasper Kane and chemical engineer John McKeen worked together during World War II and came up with a way to mass-produce the

Strong materials used to create artificial knees and replace hips have been developed through chemical engineering.

medication penicillin. Penicillin is an antibiotic that gets rid of infection-causing bacteria.

Engineers are also behind the gelcap, a medical pill that is coated with gelatin that allows for easy swallowing. The work of the chemical engineer is key in the advancement of medicine.

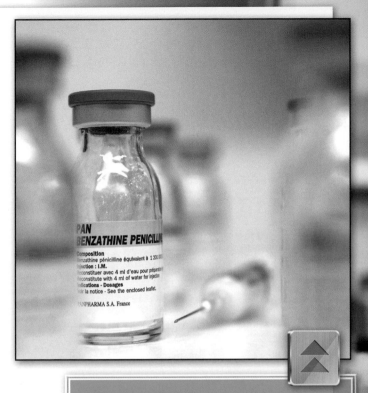

THINK ABOUT IT

Look at the list of ingredients of some medicines in your bathroom cabinet. What do you think they do?

During World War II, penicillin was used to fight infections in soldiers. A chemist and chemical engineer found a way to mass-produce the drug.

RESEARCH TO GET CHARGED UP ABOUT

Batteries are a common household item. Advancements in battery technology have largely come from chemical engineers. Chemical engineer Lewis Urry invented the alkaline battery in the late 1950s. He used a mix of zinc and manganese-dioxide. This is the battery that so many flashlights, toys, and gadgets use today. He also made the lithium battery, which is rechargeable and used in some cell phones.

Common alkaline batteries provide energy through a mix of zinc and manganese dioxide. Many electronic devices and toys would not work without batteries.

THINK ABOUT IT

Chemical engineers are trying to think of ways to make longer-lasting batteries. How long does your phone battery or laptop battery last?

Lithium-ion batteries and nickel-metal hydride batteries are used to power electric cars and laptop computers. Today's chemical engineers are looking to develop new battery technology to hold more power for longer periods of time.

Batteries may be key to building a world of cleaner energy. Batteries can be used as the back-up system for renewable energy. They can be used to store the excess electricity that is generated by solar or wind power. When this stored energy is needed, the batteries then release it.

Chemical engineers have come up with batteries used to power mobile phones and laptops.

21

Perfectly Popular Plastics

One of the most important uses of chemical engineering is in the creation of plastics. Plastics include soda bottles, toys, furniture, light switches, buttons, bubble wrap, food containers, and pipes.

The plastics industry began in 1909 with the invention of Bakelite. Bakelite was the first moldable plastic, which means it could be molded by the application of heat and pressure.

Leo Hendrik Baekeland created Bakelite. Baekeland found that his Bakelite, like all plastics, did not conduct

Plastics are one of the most widely used products. They are long-lasting, waterproof, and light— perfect for making useful products like food storage containers.

COMPARE AND CONTRAST

Plastics can be hard. Plastics can be soft. What are some of the plastics you use? Are they hard or soft?

electricity. It was used as an electric insulator for many electronics, such as radios and light-bulb sockets.

After Bakelite came along, scientists experimented and came up with many other different types of plastic.

Bakelite was the world's first human-made plastic. It was created by Leo Hendrik Baekeland.

CHEMICAL ENGINEERING IN THE COMPUTER AGE

Today, we all use and depend on computers. Integrated circuits (ICs) are key components that make computers work. Anything that is computerized or uses radio waves uses integrated circuits.

These ICs are often created from the material silicon, which is found in sand and quartz. This is why the area of computer manufacturing and development in California is called Silicon Valley.

Computers rely on integrated circuits to operate.

It takes a lot of expertise to transform silicon into integrated circuits. Chemical engineers know how to turn a silicon crystal into an integrated circuit. These circuits can also be made out of the element germanium.

The integrated circuits are key to the tiny electronics in computers and other devices. The manufacturing process of circuits has been developed by chemical engineers. Circuit production is needed to create smaller and more powerful computers.

THINK ABOUT IT

Integrated circuits are part of a computer. What do you think are some other parts? Do you think a chemical engineer might play a role in making these parts?

Chemical engineers have developed smaller and smaller integrated circuits.

WHAT DOES THE FUTURE HOLD?

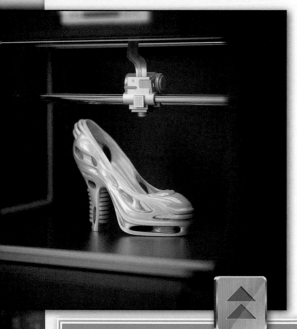

Today, 3D printers can create a wide variety of products.

Who could have dreamed that scientists would one day build a printer that could make three-dimensional (3D) objects? But today the 3D printer exists. Polymers are used to produce all sorts of objects on this type of printer, including shoes, furniture, and musical instruments.

Chemical engineers are researching new material for 3D printing. In the future, these engineers will probably be involved in finding new sources and methods for creating clean energy. They may create better fuels for space travel.

THINK ABOUT IT
What do you think chemical engineers might invent in the future?

These professionals may help industries improve the way they use chemicals to make products. They may also advise companies on ways to reduce problems such as pollution and rust.

They may work for the military making materials that are better suited for the battlefield. They will continue to come up with products that will improve human health.

Chemical engineers are always seeking ways to improve life in our modern world. For example, many are trying to find better ways to reduce pollution.

Hands-On Exercise: Making a Better Modeling Clay

It's easy to make modeling clay with flour and other ingredients.

Chemical engineers often come up with new products by mixing different things together. You can get a sense of this experience by making your own modeling clay with the help of an adult.

By combining liquids and solids, you can create something new and even fun.

Here are the basic ingredients you'll need to make your own modeling clay:

2 cups flour

2 cups warm water

1 cup salt

2 tablespoons vegetable oil

1 tablespoon cream of tartar
 *(This isn't necessary but it
 can improve elasticity)*

Food coloring *(To give your
creation some different looks)*

Put all these ingredients together in a pot and heat them slowly over a low setting on the stove. Keep stirring until the mixture gets thick like mashed potatoes.

If you can't get to a stove, you can get a claylike material without the heat. Experiment with the ingredients. What happens when you add more flour? What happens when you add more water?

You can see how a chemical engineer works by cooking flour, water, salt, and oil slowly in a pot over low heat to make modeling clay.

Glossary

chemistry A branch of science concerning the composition, structure, and properties of substances and changes they may undergo.

compound A substance formed when two or more chemical elements are bonded together.

crystalline Having a structure like a crystal. Crystals are atoms that are arranged in a rigid, geometric structure.

elasticity The ability of a material to resume its original shape after being stretched or squeezed.

element A substance that cannot be broken down into simpler substances using chemical methods.

flash freeze A process to freeze food super fast to preserve natural juices and flavors.

microscope An instrument that allows a person to view very tiny objects that cannot be seen with the eyes alone.

plastics Materials, made mostly from synthetic polymers, that can be molded into any shape by applying heat and pressure.

rubber A tough elastic substance that can be man-made or produced naturally from some trees.

semiconductor A substance that allows electricity or heat to move through it. It is often made of silicon or germanium and is used in electronics.

synthetic Artificial, or made by humans rather than occurring in nature.

technology The application of science to solve a problem or to invent a useful tool, especially for industry and commerce.

FOR MORE INFORMATION

Books

Adams, Tom. *Molecule Mayhem*. Lincolnshire, England: Templar, 2012.

Basher, Simon. *Basher Science: Chemistry: Getting a Big Reaction*. London, England: Kingfisher, 2010.

Connolly, Sean. *The Book of Totally Irresponsible Science: 64 Daring Experiments for Young Scientists*. New York, NY: Workman Publishing, 2008.

Gray, Theodore. *Molecules: The Elements and the Architecture of Everything*. New York, NY: Black Dog & Leventhal Publishers, 2014.

Stimus, John. *The Beginner's Guide to Engineering: Chemical Engineering*. North Charleston, SC: CreateSpace, 2013.

VanCleave, Janice. *Janice VanCleave's Engineering for Every Kid: Easy Activities That Make Learning Science Fun*. Hoboken, NJ: John Wiley & Sons, 2007.

Websites

Because of the changing nature of Internet links, Rosen Publishing has developed an online list of websites related to the subject of this book. This site is updated regularly. Please use this link to access the list:

http://www.rosenlinks.com/LFO/Chem

INDEX